Bodies of Art, Bodie

Bodies of Art, Bodies of Labour

Kate Beaton

UNIVERSITY of ALBERTA PRESS

Centre for Literatures in Canada
Centre de littératures au Canada

Published by

University of Alberta Press
1-16 Rutherford Library South
11204 89 Avenue NW
Edmonton, Alberta, Canada   T6G 2J4
amiskwaciwâskahikan | Treaty 6 |
Métis Territory
ualbertapress.ca | uapress@ualberta.ca

and

Centre for Literatures in Canada /
Centre de littératures au Canada
4-115 Humanities Centre
University of Alberta
Edmonton, Alberta, Canada   T6G 2E5
www.uab.ca/clc

Copyright © 2025 Kate Beaton
Introduction © 2025 Julie Rak

Library and Archives Canada
Cataloguing in Publication

Title: Bodies of art, bodies of labour /
    Kate Beaton.
Names: Beaton, Kate, 1983– author |
    University of Alberta Press, publisher.
    | Centre for Literatures in Canada,
    publisher.
Series: Henry Kreisel lecture series.
Description: Series statement: CLC Kreisel
    lecture | Includes bibliographical
    references.
Identifiers: Canadiana (print) 20240527305 |
    Canadiana (ebook) 2024052733X |
    ISBN 9781772128000 (softcover) |
    ISBN 9781772128185 (EPUB) |
    ISBN 9781772128192 (PDF)
Subjects: LCSH: Arts, Canadian—Nova
    Scotia—Cape Breton Island. | LCSH: Art
    and society—Nova Scotia—Cape Breton
    Island. | LCSH: Working class in art. |
    LCSH: Working class—Nova Scotia—
    Cape Breton Island. | LCSH: Poor—Nova
    Scotia—Cape Breton Island.
Classification: LCC NX650.L32 B43 2025 |
    DDC 305.5/62097169—dc23

First edition, first printing, 2025.
First printed and bound in Canada by
Houghton Boston Printers, Saskatoon
Saskatchewan.
Copyediting and proofreading by
Joanne Muzak.

University of Alberta Press is committed to
protecting our natural environment. As part
of our efforts, this book is printed on Enviro
Paper: it contains 100% post-consumer
recycled fibres and is acid- and chlorine-free.

GPSR: Easy Access System Europe |
Mustamäe tee 50, 10621 Tallinn, Estonia |
gpsr.requests@easproject.com

The Centre for Literatures in Canada
acknowledges the support of Dr. Eric Schloss
and the Faculty of Arts for the CLC Kreisel
Lecture delivered by Kate Beaton in March
2024 at the University of Alberta.

University of Alberta Press gratefully
acknowledges the support received for its
publishing program from the Government of
Canada, the Canada Council for the Arts, and
the Government of Alberta through the Alberta
Media Fund.

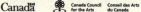

Foreword

The CLC's Henry Kreisel Memorial Lecture is an annual event that fosters public and scholarly engagement with pressing issues faced by Canadian writers. Each year, a distinguished author is invited to explore a topic that is significant to them, whether it reflects a personal passion, a foundational aspect of their work, or an issue of our particular cultural moment. Covering important themes such as oppression, social justice, cultural identity, displacement, censorship, multilingualism, literary history, Indigenous resurgence, anti-racist poetics, and the vital role of art, these lectures enrich our understanding of life and literary culture in Canada. Held before a live audience on Treaty 6 Territory and Region 4 of the Métis Nation of Alberta at the University of Alberta campus, several Kreisel Lectures have also been broadcast nationally as episodes of CBC Radio One's *Ideas* program. Each lecture is subsequently published as a book in collaboration with University of Alberta Press.

In March 2024 Kate Beaton, the widely acclaimed author of *Ducks: Two Years in the Oil Sands*, delivered the 18th Kreisel Lecture to a full house at Edmonton's Timms Centre for the Arts. Beaton immersed her audience in the textures of life in Cape Breton, a "have-not" region of Canada whose cultural history highlights the profound impact that class has on the arts. A neglected topic in most institutional discussions of literature and culture, class, as Beaton amply shows, dramatically affects who can become a practicing artist, limiting the choices people can make and the paths they can take, from their educational opportunities to how and where they can work. Beaton's meticulously researched and moving lecture weaves together the story of her own journey as an artist struggling to make a living and pay off student debt, with a poignant critique of the histories of (mis)representation that have objectified her community and its regional culture. Thus, the author and renowned cartoonist not only illuminates an important context for her graphic memoir *Ducks*, but also makes a powerful argument for self-representation and the importance of supporting artists financially.

The Centre for Literatures in Canada (CLC) was established in 2006 with a founding gift from noted Edmontonian bibliophile and comics collector Dr. Eric Schloss and his wife, Elexis, both of whom are members of the Order of Canada. In 2007 this lecture series was established in honour of Professor Henry Kreisel. Author, University Professor, and Officer of the Order of Canada, Kreisel was born into a Jewish family in Vienna in 1922. He left his homeland for England in 1938 and was interned in Canada for eighteen months during the Second World War. After studying at the University of Toronto, he was hired in 1947 to teach at the University of Alberta, where he was the Chair of English from 1961 to 1970. He served as Vice-President (Academic) from 1970 to 1975, when he was named University Professor, the highest scholarly award bestowed on its faculty members by the University of Alberta. An inspiring and beloved teacher who taught generations of students to appreciate literature, Professor Kreisel was among the first to champion Canadian literature in university classrooms and, through his own writing, to bring the experience of immigrants to modern Canadian literature. Kreisel was also an early advocate for Indigenous research and scholarship at the University of Alberta, working to build bridges between Indigenous communities and the university. His written works include two novels, *The Rich Man* (1948) and *The Betrayal* (1964), and a collection of short stories, *The Almost Meeting* (1981). His internment diary, alongside critical essays on his writing, appears in *Another Country: Writings by and about Henry Kreisel* (1985). He died in Edmonton in 1991. The generosity and foresight of Professor Kreisel's teaching at the University of Alberta continues to inspire the CLC in its research pursuits, public outreach, and ongoing commitment to the ever-growing richness, complexity, and diversity of literatures in Canada.

Sarah Wylie Krotz
Director, Centre for Literatures in Canada /
Centre de littératures au Canada
Edmonton, June 2024

Introduction
Julie Rak

Kate Beaton is having a moment, in Canada and beyond. It's such an honour to introduce one of my favourite comics creators, who has made an instant classic that resonates with so many people, in Canada and everywhere else, in the world of comics and in the rest of the world. *Ducks*, the story of Beaton's quest in 2005 to pay off her student loans by leaving her home in Cape Breton, Nova Scotia, to work in the oilfields of Northern Alberta, is *the* autobiographical comic to read. The story was universally well reviewed in 2023, and it won best artist and best graphic memoir at the Eisner Awards, the most significant awards in the comics industry. It even became the first graphic book to win the CBC annual Canada Reads contest, defended brilliantly by *Jeopardy!* super-champion and fellow Maritimer, Mattea Roach. With that win, *Ducks* made the jump from the alternative comics scene—where Beaton is well known for her web comics and her collection *Hark! A Vagrant*—to mainstream fame. This is really something for the creator of sexy Batman and the sendups of Nancy Drew book covers you find in *Hark! A Vagrant*. Of course, I still love sexy Batman. Who doesn't?

More seriously, there are many reasons why *Ducks* achieved almost immediate popular and critical success. The autobiographical comic appeared at a time when awareness of the impact of the oilfields on the economy and environment in Canada was sharply on the rise. Alberta, the province where most of the action of *Ducks* takes place, is constantly in world news because of oil production and its attendant controversies. Alberta itself is an important node of petroculture, a society built on the extraction of fossil fuels, and that takes much of its meaning and identity from the labour for and environmental impact of extraction. Most of the time, the public discourse of Alberta either figures oil as the underpinning of all economic and social life that must never be called into question, or it sees the oil and gas industry as the symbol of the environmental destruction and of economic boom/bust problems. The clash between the two points of view is usually figured in public discourse as a relatively simple choice between jobs or the environment. But there is another side to the oil and gas industry that is often disregarded as the conflict plays out: the lives of oilfield workers themselves and what it is like for them to leave their homes and work in Northern Alberta. That is what *Ducks* is really about. As Beaton eloquently points out, the production of oil is dependent on the extraction of labour from other parts of Canada and the world. Oil mining and refining takes place on land stolen from Indigenous people, another extraction. The system of extraction creates its own kinds of violence, alienation, and social problems, even as it brings a measure of prosperity for oilfield workers.

Beaton shows all this with the genre of autobiographical comics. It has often been pointed out in comics scholarship that hand-drawn comics can't help but be autobiographical. The creator's body, even her soul, is in every line. Comics creators *draw* themselves, and use the medium of comics to tell stories that can't be told any other way. Some of the best autobiographical comics ever produced are made in and about Canada, by artists such as Chester Brown, Julie Doucet, Seth and Jillian Tamaki. *Ducks* therefore positions itself within this tradition at the centre of ambiguity about jobs, labour, and the environment, and does not look for easy answers. It runs these huge issues through Beaton's own perspective as a young woman from a have-not region who dreams of a different kind of future for herself as she works to pay her student loans and figure out her life's work in the process. Beaton sets out to show us how there can be beauty in the midst of ugliness, sexism, and violence against women and against the land as well. In the midst of community and camaraderie, there is a longing for home that cannot, for people like her from Atlantic Canada, ever be reconciled with economic realities. "I learn that I can have opportunity or I can have home. I cannot have both, and either will always hurt," Beaton writes at the beginning of *Ducks*. The story that unfolds is a testament to the complexity of having to live with and through the realities of extraction. It is autobiographical storytelling at its finest, told by a master of comics as a medium.

Bodies
of Art,
Bodies
of Labour

// My neighbour tells a story that makes me laugh. When he was a kid, he and his family went to a restaurant for the first time in his life. It was very exciting. Order whatever you want. So, he ordered bread and molasses. That wasn't on the menu, and the waitress was perplexed, but that's what they ate at home. That's what everyone ate at home because it was cheap, and no one had any money. We laugh because this is a child's social gaffe, you are supposed to order off the menu, you are supposed to know.

This is a talk about class. I can think of lots of times in my own life where I just did not *know* what I was supposed to know, according to those above me, and how that felt. But it works both ways. The knowledge deficit is on the other side as well.

There is a famous history book from 1963 by E.P. Thompson called *The Making of the English Working Class*. It was the big bang for popular history from the bottom up, instead of the "great man" type of history. Its most famous quote is when Thompson says that he seeks to rescue poor workers "from the enormous condescension of posterity."[1] It's a good phrase, and the subtext is that posterity belongs to the upper class. It's another way of saying the oft-quoted "history is written by the victors," which I think is a quote mostly trotted out bitterly from the point of view of the losing side. We all feel our losses keenly. And so I say, as someone from the working class, that posterity in the arts belongs largely to the affluent. Not just success on a personal level but the accumulation of people who have come from generational wealth vs. those who do not. The people who create the bulk of what we consume and accept as our own culture over years. "The enormous condescension of posterity." Yes. That'll do.

A few years ago, the Canada Council for the Arts published a large survey—a *Statistical Profile of Artists in Canada*.[2] The survey had information on a wide range of demographics: career profiles, age, gender, current income, education, ethnicity, immigration status, language, and employment. However, Canada Council had nothing to say on class background. They have been under fire for being a classist organization from the get-go, so I must say I was a little surprised.

Another survey: In 2022 the Association of Canadian Publishers produced the *Canadian Book Publishing Industry Diversity Baseline Survey*.[3] The results were about people working in the publishing industry and had a lot to say about where they worked in Canada, what age, what type of work they did, if they had a disability, what department they worked in, what race they identified as, what gender, what sexual orientation, their salary, type of contract, and who held what positions of authority. Again, there was nothing on class background.

Perhaps that is a metric that is too hard to measure, too vague to define. Class is a system of ordering people based on social or economic status, and also *perceived* social or economic status. Perhaps it is asking too much to draw a line between classes when there are so many intersectionalities that permeate what we think of when we think of class, muddying an already hard-to-define status.

I suppose we do have the low income cut-off, which is a solid number and other government socioeconomic benchmarks if we need them. And there is even just the feeling that yes, I was raised working class. It's not all about money after all, it's about where you're from, what your community looks like, what informs your tastes, what gives you the shorthand with which to navigate and network—or be unable to network—the social world around you or above you, as it were. You know who you are. But maybe that is not good enough.

However, even with all of those arguments and reasons to hedge around class, there is no denying that class is a reality in people's lives with enormous consequence. These surveys are just one example of the ways in which we ignore class in Canada when it could be part of the conversation.

How can you define something that is made to be invisible to begin with? For the purpose of this talk, I should define for you what I mean when I say "working class." It is an elastic term, even in my view. There is no one definition that satisfies. It was once the proletariat, people who only had their labour to sell as economic value, but not anymore. It used to mean people without post-secondary degrees, but many workers have those, or they have occupation-specific training. It used to conjure images of factories but most working-class people today are in the service industry.[4] To cut off the working class from the poor and the middle class by one income amount each feels arbitrary to individual experience. I think self-identification is what makes it: "We work but we are poor, we are working class."

Even that has its issues. Wolfgang Lehmann, sociology professor at Western University, often found his subjects (working-class students) unable to name themselves as, in fact, working class. Even when there were obvious signifiers, as in they were the first in their families to go to university and their parents were mechanics and beauticians. When asked, they supposed they might be middle class, by virtue of having grown up in a house and having employed parents.[5]

These sentiments are backed up by the research. In 2023 the Angus Reid Institute published a large study on class in Canada.[6] It found that most Canadians do not think or talk that much about social class, and, most of us, for better or worse, consider ourselves as hewing towards the middle class, whether we are below it or above it. And isn't that who politicians are always talking to anyway? The average Canadian? But that same study also points out that class mobility is difficult in real life—even though Canadians believe in meritocracy, believe in getting ahead through hard work—it is hard to get from the bottom to the top. Yet class division has always been central to our national makeup, whether we acknowledge it or not. Often, not. This is true in the arts as much as anywhere.

Economist Karol Jan Borowiecki did a survey of 160 years of US demographic data.[7] It told the obvious, but it showed it on paper: If you come from more money, you are more likely to be an artist than someone who did not.

Someone whose family has an annual income of $100,000 is twice as likely to become an artist, actor, musician, or author than anyone else from a family with an income of $50,000. If you raise that income to $1 million, they are ten times more likely to be an artist.

It is easy to understand why—to leap into a creative field is to walk into the arms of an industry that might not love you back, financially. The stakes are high for someone with no money. If there is no one to catch you when you fall, it is a choice you just can't make. You can only be a starving artist if you or your family is not actually, literally, starving.

The New York Times added a little finesse to this data with its own study of surveys, finding in 2017 that way more young people pursuing an art career get a financial bump from their parents, and a higher amount of it, compared to their blue-collar peers.[8]

In short, the arts is full of more people who came from wealthier backgrounds than not, people who in turn decide what stories are told, whose voices are heard, and, in essence, who decides what our culture is. If class is not a part of the rubric of demographics, of what we expect when we think of intersectionality and representation, then we are missing something critical. We are not looking for distinct voices that make up a large portion of this country. We need to talk about class.

// I have been aware of class my entire life. My parents worked very hard for very little, but, they would be the first to point out, it's not like anyone else had anything either. That's life in a working-class community.

As a child, you accept your life as normal whatever the circumstances. If you have no money, it doesn't matter that nothing looks like the houses on TV, nothing is ever new, and toy commercials mean nothing because, well, *dream on*. But you still know what's going on. If parents have anxiety over what to spend money on, kids are the first to tune in. As I am discovering now because I have a four-year-old and a two-year-old, kids are always listening.

Class is there, in the background. When you get older, though, when you start to make your way in the wider world, class reveals itself in sharp relief. Especially in all the ways that you are found lacking. The connections you don't have. The skills you never learned. The accent you speak with. The way you look. And, of course, the money you don't have, and possibly never will. When I speak about class, this is really how I understand it. This is how I know what I am.

Today, I am a cartoonist. That means I am a writer and an artist and an illustrator. I get to do it all. I wanted, so badly, to be an artist from a very young age. But I'm from a have-not place. At that young age, I had no resources; I didn't have the tools to navigate the system I thought I needed to become what I wanted so badly. My village was small and my school only had so much. They were used to sending the bright students off to teaching and nursing degrees, sensible choices in a place with limited options. The last thing they wanted was to set us up for failure by sending us into a career like the arts, when they knew there was little they could do to help us, and no money at home to carve a way to success. I said I wanted to be an animator, and I think the guidance counsellor and I both started sweating.

It was demoralizing. I recall a sad scene in the small village museum where I worked in the summer. My father came to drop off the university course packet that came in the mail, but the course packet was not the one I longed for. I was going for a bachelor of arts instead of the fine arts or animation degree I had dreamed of for years. With a BA you can always be a teacher or a lawyer so, keep your doors open. Always keep your doors open. My father was proud to drop off the university mail, but I wept for my broken seventeen-year-old dreams and he didn't know what do to.

What were my parents supposed to think anyway? They were nothing but supportive and proud, but they came from an even harder reality than I did. When my mother's oldest sister went away for work, the first thing she did with her money was install a bathroom in the old house. Imagine the luxury you think your kids have when you didn't even have a bathroom. The first thing I did with my money, of course, was pay off my own fancy education.

No print market would have wanted me when I started making comics. I was working in a camp in an oil sands mine; I was a woman from a poor town making crude-looking drawings on my time off because I had twelve-hour shifts, and I wasn't even that familiar with comics. Rural poor places didn't have them. I never had an art class, and it showed. Nobody would have wanted me. I can smell the rejection letters baking in the oven.

I had one stroke of fortune. The internet was, at that time anyway, a great equalizer. There were no gatekeepers. It was like jumping the turnstiles to get on the train. You just made things and put them up and anyone in the world could look at them. And I was making these jokey comics about history and literature and things I was interested in, something I started at the university student newspaper but started to post online after I graduated. People who also liked those things responded in kind. It felt so good to be seen. I was doing it for nothing, for the joy of it. My day job was in a mine and living in a work camp; there was harassment and isolation and pollution and drugs and so many other things. But I would post these comics at night and people would see me as I wanted to be seen, and that was worth so much.

Then someone else who was making comics online in the same way started a company that sold merchandise for people's websites and invited me to be part of it so that I could make an income, and I did.[9] And though my career has changed a lot, I have been making a living from comics since 2008. It is a great shame that the window of time where the internet was as open as it was when I came in shifted and shrank and you can't do it that way anymore.

I did get published eventually, after I was legitimized by popularity. Got an agent, the works. But it wasn't just me who came in through the back door to get there. Without gatekeepers, the internet brought down class barriers but it also gave similar entry and acclaim to queer people, racialized people, people telling stories that felt unmarketable or unprintable. Today, comics, which used to be synonymous with white men, is one of the most diverse mediums we have.

Now, being one of the rare artists who manages to come from the working class and make a living from creative work alone, I want to reflect on representation of people like me in literature where I am from. I can't speak for class broadly, as it spans the continent, but I can speak for myself, and I can tell you that representation—or lack of it—has an effect. It empowers and edifies you, or it stereotypes and diminishes you, or worse, it erases you.

I said before that there are those who decide what our culture is, but behind that idea is another one, a request, a need we have. Culture should belong to everyone, with the same authenticity and power.

It does not always work out that way.

// Let's go back, way way back, to 1886. There's a travel article from *Harper's New Monthly Magazine* out of New York by one Charles H. Farnham.[10] He's come to Cape Breton to get out of the "fizz and flash" of the city (his words) and look at people the way they used to live. Simple people who aren't spoiled by modern noise. The article is "Cape Breton Folk."

The thing about looking for something specific is that if you go that far to get it, your mind is made up and you might convince yourself you have found it no matter what you see. Farnham wants to see simple people, and so, simple people he sees. He takes a lot in. Wakes, marriages, festivals, scenery. Then he gets to my village, and suddenly the scenery isn't so scenic. They are driving over a cape and it's high and windy, and little rocks are tumbling into the water far below. The wind is demonic. He says it is all personified by a poor old man who is trying to farm something: "The life of the region seemed to be personated by a withered old man, whose ragged homespun hung on him as on a skeleton, and whose unkempt locks flew about with the wind. He bent low over his scythe, and with tragic eagerness tried to mow the few spears of wiry grass sticking up out of the barren earth. A little more steepness, and he had rolled into the sea as the stones did; a little more wind, and he had been whirled away as the leaves in November." He continues, "Night seemed more in harmony with such bleak poverty than the glory of sunset; it enshrouded us all as we threaded our way homeward, inland, up one of the glens." He makes his way to the next town: "Whycocomagh was doubly charming after the bleakness of the sea-coast and the fatigue of travel...I settled down in the comfortable inn to continue my rambles in Cape Breton throughout the Indian summer. It is one of the prettiest places on the island."[11] He had to look at poor people, yuck! Haha. That made him sad! Sad as the NIGHT. He came to see delightful wee simple folk, not like, gross poverty. But he woke up in a charming inn in a more affluent village so that made things better. New day, new adventures for our man Charles.

I'm going to pause here and we will put a pin in the withered old man in ragged homespun holding a scythe, the poor man in my home village. I don't want you to feel too bad for my forebears. Not even the ragged man on the cliff. The village in which Charles Farnham landed and found a comfortable inn at the end of that passage was Whycocomagh, about a thirty-minute drive from my house right now. He finds it, as says, beautiful and prosperous. But this is Canada, and in Canada we should know that the darker truth is underneath that.

The truth here was that Whycocomagh, beautiful as it was, was an Indigenous settlement, a Mi'kmaw reserve, but it had been encroached on and taken by white squatters who cared neither about the fact that Cape Breton (Unama'ki) was unceded land as a whole, or that the reservation specifically was not theirs. Around that time, estimates suggest half of Cape Breton was settled via squatting: the settlers either had no money to petition for land, or the system was not set up to accommodate them, so they squatted. Chief Peter Googoo of Whycocomagh wrote a petition to the lieutenant governor of Nova Scotia in 1855 appealing for help because squatters were taking land that was precious to them, some of it already cultivated, and they were in fear of their future.[12]

No help came. But another petition came out two years later, this one from the settlers themselves, asking the government for more of the Mi'kmaw land—because, in their opinion, they were best suited to civilize the area, and the Natives were dying anyway.[13]

Today we acknowledge that we are on unceded Indigenous land nationwide. But we are still entrenched in a racialized society harmed by the violence of colonialism. The third signature on that second petition is a Beaton. I don't know who he is, but he is a potent reminder of who I am. Heir of the colonizer, beneficiary of the system they created. Class does not exist alone. It has many bedfellows, and race is the most intertwined among them. There is no talking about class without talking about race.

To talk to you about class from my perspective, I can't give voice to the experience of being racialized. That is a double barrel of society's treatment I have not had to look down. I'm white, with a settler history two hundred years long. But I know that history. Everything I have, love, and cherish comes from the moment some-one came off a boat and squatted on land that was never theirs. Everyone was poor, but this is the truth about class as well: poor white people have always been the first in line, class wise, to receive the benefit of the doubt, the leg up, the open door, the extended hand. I have benefit-ted from that fact as sure as I am standing here in front of you.

Side note: The Indigenous settlement of Whycocomagh is now We'koqma'q First Nation and it is currently situated directly alongside the village of Whycocomagh, the village that consumed their land. For decades, they have been trying to address the issue of stolen land that was taken from them by squatters and ignored by the govern-ment. It is not yet rectified. But it is their land. And this is not to vilify one village, because this happened every-where, and the theft, violence, or indifference involved in settler acquisition of Indigenous land is barely acknowledged.

And though I can't tell you personal things outside my experience, I can tell you some more facts. More facts! That Canada Council arts survey found that racialized

Canadians are under-represented among artists (15%) compared with all workers (21%).[14] Indigenous and immigrant workers are slightly under-represented among artists. These facts can sit independently of class, but often there is a relationship.

And remember that 2022 Association of Canadian Publishers *Canadian Book Publishing Industry Diversity Baseline Survey*? Well, it didn't account for class in the publishing industry, but it did note that 75 per cent of respondents were white, an overwhelming majority.[15] Seventy per cent of the population ticked the last national census as white, but not in the big cities like Toronto and Vancouver, where it is more like 40 per cent.[16] So, 70 per cent of the Canadian population coast to coast might be white, but I don't know many publishing houses in the corn cob fields in Ontario. They're in places more likely to be diverse.

I'm not saying this is a "gotcha" moment. Sure, the publishing figures look only slightly higher than the national ones. I just think there are different ways of looking at the statistics. Bias is like Waldo—he's on every page, if you look. He wears a little hat and glasses.

More figures: "Non-white" is not a group, of course. If you look at these surveys, you'll find other things—like, in the Canadian census, 4.3 per cent of the population is Black.[17] But in the publishing survey, only 2.6 per cent of responders were Black.[18] Half the size. Those differences matter. They tell a story.

The most diverse department in all of publishing? Perhaps unsurprisingly, it is interns, the newest and lowest paid of all, as well as the ones who may not make it career wise.[19]

Let's go back to the pin.

// It's 1886 and the ragged man with the scythe has put Charles Farnham off his lunch. He is attempting to mow a few spears from the barren earth before the wind blows his skeletal frame into the sea. Charles departs for greener pastures. The man is left where he is. He has no interiority; he is just tragic.

This kind of travel writing is common about Cape Breton, and we will get more into that. But by its very nature, travel writing is all about looking at things, and the main character is the writer. We are given an interpretation of what is seen and experienced through the writer's lens. Travel writing assigns value through the writer's value. It can only give you so much.

The man had interiority, a family, a community, a culture. And in a way, we can let him speak for himself. I don't know who this man is, but I can introduce you to my great, great, great-grandfather. His name was Aonghas mac Alasdair, and he was a bard, a poet. He was born in Mabou in 1817, where I too was born, 166 years later.

We are lucky that any of his songs survived. He was not fluent in English; Gaelic was his tongue, as was the case for many in the area. He was a protégé of Allan "the Ridge" MacDonald, famous poet of the region, though I understand your mileage on "famous" may vary. But Allan was famous enough, and when he left the village and the two poets parted ways, Aonghas bought his farm. And it was, unfortunately, kind of a shitty farm. To be fair, the crop blight of the 1840s was making all farming difficult and hard to get out from under. And so Aonghas, poor and blighted, put pen to paper and wrote "Òran do Ghaiseadh a' Bharra"—"The Crop Failure Song."

Òran do Ghaiseadh a' Bharra

Air fonn: Cogadh no sìth.

Bho'n rinn mi 'n seo dìreadh 's ann chinn mi cho fann
Leis na fhuair mi do mhìmhadh 's na tìmean a th'ann;
'S gun dad dhomh le fìrinn a' cinntinn ach clann,
Gun d' sheachainn mi 'm prìosan le innleachd mo làimh.

Gun d'chuir mi 'm buntàta am pàirc ann an sloc
Gun d' dhubh e cho tràth ann 's nach d' fhàs e ach olc;
An cruithneachd cha d' fhàs e 's an t-àilean cho bochd
'S ma chreideas mi 'n tàillear, tha fàilinn sa choirc'.

Thug an t-earchall an sprèidh bhuam 's cha lèir dhomh
    carson
Gun d' ghoid e gu lèir iad, gun seud air an son,
Ach seich' air a reubadh aig feursainn gun toil,
'S a chuid eile de 'n chreubhaig gu lèir aig na coin.

Se gaiseadh a' bharra dh'fhàg falamh mo phòc'
Cha tèid mi bho 'n bhaile 's gun agam an gròt;
Ged dh'èireadh gun tachradh orm caraid 's tigh-òsd'
'S fheudar dol dhachaigh 's gun farraid air stòp.

Ged thèid mi 'n tigh-òsda chan òl mi ann dràm
Chan iarr iad mo chòmhradh 's mo phòca cho gann;
Na bonnanan bòidheach bu chòir a bhith ann
Chan fhaigh mi ri òl iad 's gun stòl mi gun taing.

A bhean a' freagairt:

'Se dh'iarras mi nis ort, dèan driosgag dheth òl
Cha dèan e do bhristeadh 's bidh glic ann a' seòl;
Gum pàigh sinn na shir sinn 's bidh misnich ri d' bheò,
Tha botal 'sa chistidh 's cha mhisde sinn òl.

Gun d' shuidh mi gu socrach 's am botal am làimh
'S gun dh' òl mi deoch thodaidh chuir sogan nam cheann;
Cha robh taobh air an nochdainn nach e fortan a bh' ann
'S gun d' fhuadaich e bhochdainn mu 'n do chosg sinn na
   bh' ann!

The Crop Failure Song

Since I moved up here, I have become feeble due to the
hardships I have undergone these times. Indeed I am
unable to produce anything but children—and I have only
avoided debtors' prison by dint of my handwork.

I planted potatoes in a hollow in the field but they blackened so early and only grew poorly; the wheat did not
grow because the meadow was so infertile—and if I
believe the Tailor, the oats are also failing.

Disease took my cattle, I cannot fathom why—it took
them all without a cent for them; all that was left were
hides torn and riddled with worms while the rest of the
carcass went to the dogs.

It was the crop blight that left my pockets empty; I can't
leave the farm as I don't have a groat. Though I might
meet a friend in the tavern, I must head home without
ordering a (stoup) pint.

Though I might go to the tavern, I won't have a dram
there—they don't want my company since my pockets are so empty; I cannot spend the bonny coins that
should be there on drink so I have to settle regardless.

His wife answers him:

I will now invite you to have a drop which won't beggar
you, and you be wise about it; we will pay all we
requested and you be optimistic always, there's a bottle
in the chest and we won't be the worse for drinking it.

So I sat down comfortably with bottle in hand and drank
a toddy which cheered my mind; everywhere I looked
there was only good fortune, and poverty was banished
by the time we finished it off![20]

These are really hard times. He is not flinching away
from the reality of poverty and the devastating effects of
the crop failure that gives the song its title. The potatoes
blackened, the wheat and oats won't grow, disease takes
the cattle. But there is humour here. He wants a drink at
the tavern and he can't have it, there's no money. Then
his wife winks and pulls a bottle from the chest and says,
"Chin up." He pours himself a good one and everywhere
he looks, it's good fortune and poverty is gone!

But the line that gets me is when he says, in rough
translation, "things are so bad here that I can't grow
anything but children." Indeed, he had nine of them. It's
a funny line. You wouldn't suppose there was humour
through hardship if all you had was a travel writer's brief
disdain. But let people speak for themselves.

Of course, of these two accounts of poverty in Mabou
at that time, one was published by a writer in a famous
magazine we all recognize the name of, which you can
find even now if you google it. It has wider cultural cachet
no matter how archival it becomes. The other is only
housed physically in the Special Collections of St. Francis

Xavier University's Celtic Studies Department, and in the museum in Mabou, and in memory.

If I wanted to understand what life was like at the time, I wouldn't have to look hard for one, but I would have to look very, very hard for the other. Even 150 years later, class is power.

// There is a funny reoccurrence in medieval bestiaries: elephants. A lot of the artists who drew the bestiaries had never seen an elephant—why would they, they were European monks who lived in monasteries—but they were charged with producing the image of one based on what they were told. So, you know, you have a greyish four-legged animal, large with big ears, two enormous tusks, a tail, and, most curious of all, a long, long nose. Like a trumpet? Like a hose? I don't know.

What would your drawing look like if you knew what an elephant looked like but you didn't *know* what an elephant *looked like*? The answer is, of course, bizarre. Anything between a giant pig, horse, dog, or boar, with something ridiculous coming out of its face. The modern viewer knows it is a drawing of an elephant, but also, they know it is not a drawing of an elephant.

This is how I feel sometimes looking at portrayals of the working class or of poor people when they are written by someone who is just going off of what they have heard. Those middle-class writers who give us so many of our lower-class characters. They are writing off of an idea, and other images and books and media they have consumed that told them "this is the way it is."

They don't need to live it; they have the authority that comes with looking down. How many more depictions of poor people do we need to see how their economic status, their poverty, is a personal failure instead of a systematic one? It is inherent in how they are bad parents, addicted to something, lazy, or stupid, or dirty, or crude, or violent compared to their middle-class counterparts.

How many times are they an object of ridicule? How many times have we looked into a working-class home on television or a movie and seen a bleak hole where a family should be? No, you don't want to live there.

Defined by everything they do not have, according to their betters. You maybe want to hear about the one who escaped all this, not the ones who live it. The one who is palatable is the one who is different from all the rest. And it is all about what reinforces a sense of superiority, what brings on pity, or disgust instead of a social conscious-ness of other people's circumstances. And how can we reveal a truer culture, with empathy and understanding of one another, without a real understanding of each other's circumstances?

If there is no authentic representation, then all you will have are medieval drawings of elephants.

// Earlier generations of writing about Cape Breton did not trade so much in the stereotypes of lower classes we have now—people as failures—they had a different image in mind. That of the Folk. What do I mean by the Folk? Well, let's get into it.

There is a seminal work from 1994 called *Quest of the Folk* by Ian McKay that has influenced all writing on literature around Atlantic Canada since it was published.[21]

It is hard to find a bibliography without it. *Quest of the Folk* comes for us all, and it came for me on a sylla-bus in an anthropology folklore course in university.

It is so popular because it lays bare the machine that helped create Nova Scotia as a place of mythic Folk ideal. That of the backwards rural people, simple, friendly, and pre-industrial, living in a golden age the rest of the country is sentimental for, ready to be discovered.

Charles Farnham was not first, nor the last, to land on the Nova Scotia shore in search of simple people living a simple life somewhere back in time.

McKay's book goes heavy in the ring with folklorist Helen Creighton, who scoured rural Nova Scotia for folk songs and folklore during her career in the early twentieth century, but selected for publication only that which she deemed authentic and appropriate and to her taste. That taste was very conservative and sanitized, and racially selective. Her work was very popular, and helped promote an anti-modern aesthetic for the region that the middle class and outsiders flocked to. But it did not represent the reality, which was modernizing, industrializing, racially diverse, and often cruder than she would allow.[22]

McKay argues a strong case that Nova Scotia commodified a folk culture for tourism and commercial interests, especially during the time of Premier Angus L. Macdonald, but continuing ever since. In these images and texts, the province looks bucolic, purposefully stuck in the past, often very white and particularly Scottish or Acadian, erasing Indigenous people and Black communities and other immigrant settlers. Yet the oldest Black communities in Canada are situated in Nova Scotia. In all these arguments, McKay was very on the money.

The folklorists all came from the middle class, had the equipment and the cars to drive around because they had the leisure to do so. They could publish books about what they chose to include as culture, and what they chose to omit. But we had all those books growing up that everyone else had, and I remember wishing that Creighton had come to my town, because the people in the books had a record of themselves on paper where we did not. It felt like proof of something, that's all I knew.

You also can't deny the impact of tourist literature or tourism images on how the world sees us and how we see ourselves in the world.

McKay writes of the Nova Scotia Folk, "They lived, generally, in fishing and farming communities, supposedly far removed from capitalist social relations and the stresses of modernity. The Folk did not work in factories, coal mines, lobster canneries, or domestic service: they were rooted to the soil and to the rockbound coast, and lived lives of self-sufficiency close to nature."[23]

You can conjure that in your mind, you've seen it, an east coast postcard. Beautiful. It's a powerful image. And a pervasive one. But if that was who we were, if that is how the rest of the country saw us, as backward rural simpletons, then you know how it affected the way people were allowed to live their lives.

Should those people, in that image, make decisions for themselves? No. They're too backwards. Should they aspire to more? No. They are stuck where they are, and they like it. Should they have a voice? No. Better educated people should talk for them. The Maritime provinces are always being accused of being too sentimental for their own good, as if that, at its core, wasn't also something partially manufactured and put on them by people who wanted it that way.

I think Cape Breton has also just always existed in the imagination of people in and outside of all this as a refuge from modernity, by its very geography. Look at it on a map. Islands carry their own romance, and there, on the edge of the continent, this looks like a place to get away from it all.

In the 1950s, Timothy Asch, a young anthropologist (not a tourist), who would later become famous in his field, was sent to my village to document the way people used to live, because there, "they still live that way."[24] They were an official control group for the past.

So, let's go on a trip.

A friend of mine handed me a book by Edna Staebler called *Cape Breton Harbour*. This book, published in 1972, chronicles Staebler's visit to Neil's Harbour, a Cape Breton fishing village.[25]

Staebler was a well-known Canadian journalist from Kitchener, Ontario. She wrote for publications like *Chatelaine*, but is best known for a cookbook titled *Food That Really Schmecks*.[26] She helped found the literary journal *The New Quarterly* along with Farley Mowat and Harold Horwood. Wilfrid Laurier University has a creative writing award in her name.

But in 1948, she was yet unpublished and visiting Cape Breton, taking notes for what would be her first ever published article—a piece for *Maclean's* magazine about Neil's Harbour that would jumpstart her career.[27] The book about this visit was published years later, as I said, in 1972. Among all of her writing, she said it was her favourite.

It's an interesting book to read today. Not because it is famous, but because of the way it is written, and how much she shows her hand. Staebler was coming to the island on vacation. She may have been writing about 1948, but this book was published only a decade before I was born. The copy on the back jacket—the marketing— tells you a lot immediately: "The spell of the sea will be on you as you read this finely illustrated story of Edna Staebler's discovery of a fishing village on the Cabot Trail. Like a seashell, or a pocket full of sand, the book will talk to you of people, the sound of gulls and the sea, long after you have read it...She grew to love the people, who in turn accepted her into their lives. Here is an intimate look at what many people mean when they think of 'the Maritimes.'" Well, that certainly paints a picture. It evokes McKay's "the Folk," to be sure. It is a dust jacket written for the middle class to come out of the city and "discover" something more primitive.

When she lands in Neil's Harbour, she thinks it is ugly and poor and the food is bad. She learns quickly to love and appreciate it, and that is, you might say, the point of the book. However, we as the reader take what we are given, we are told it is a dump right away and so we have to believe it. Especially if we are the Upper Canadian middle class to whom this book is marketed. When she says, "I certainly won't stay here a week; I won't even unpack my bags. The red Malcolm woman is hostile, the fishermen might be filthy old men and I wouldn't be safe in their boats, the glitter on the sea is menacing,"[28] what are we supposed to think? She changes her mind, sure, but we are never not looking at these people and this place the way she is looking at them.

An interesting feature of the book is that for its entire length, the local people speak in phonetic dialogue, with their accents painstakingly spelled out. Not every single word, but also it is happening all the time. This is done in the name of authenticity, or as her contemporaries would put it, immersive journalism.

Another boy cut out the bloody eye socket, looked inquiringly at me, then grinned and tossed it into the water.

"How much would the fish weigh?" I asked anyone who could hear me.

"Ower six hundred pound, I reckon," a blue-eyed fish-erman answered. "He's some beeg."

"What does it taste like?"

"Don't know, never et 'em, we just ketches 'em and sells 'em for folks down in States," he said. "Don't fancy to try none o' the big ugly things meself but some round 'ere cut off a bit near the haid and taked it home and cooked it; they say hit's got a roight noice flavour to it, loike pork, not strong atall. Americans must loike 'em or they wouldn't pay so much for 'em. We's gettin' thirty-two cents a pound today."

I did some mental arithmetic. "No wonder you're so happy to catch one."

He grinned. "We be, but they's awful scarce." With a saw in his hand he knelt beside the fish. "Want sword?" he asked me.

"Oh yes. Don't you need it?"

He laughed. "We just throws 'em overboard."[29]

Pierre Berton said, "Edna immerses herself in her story... She becomes part of the narrative. She lives the lives of the people she writes about; she listens to their prob-lems and they become her friends."[30] To Berton, she broke boundaries.

She did break boundaries. She was a pioneer of liter-ary journalism. She was a woman in a field heavily dominated by men. And she worked hard at it. It is also clear that Staebler loved Cape Breton. Her biography makes that explicit. When her marriage was souring, she wrote in a letter to a friend, "I want much of the time to run away—to find again the joy I had when I was at Neil's Harbour."[31] She would go back, and said she felt more at home there than anywhere. Contentment. She felt welcomed. She was welcomed.

So, I do not mean to pick on poor Edna Staebler. Certainly, there are many more villainous writers who can prove the point. This is a big chunk of the twentieth century. Travel writers everywhere are gallivanting and writing things that horrify the modern eye.

Try Margaret Warner Morley's 1900 book, *Down North and Up Along*, where she, a biologist, indulges in her own personal race theory throughout.[32] Thanks, I hate it!

How about 1948's *Cape Breton, Isle of Romance* by Arthur Walworth?[33] *The New York Times* says that "it gives a leisurely, intimate view of the semi-primeval life of the Scotch, Irish, French and Micmac Indians who occupy this island."[34] This man has a Pulitzer Prize in literature! They give those to anybody.

No, Staebler is interesting to me because she is not so easily dismissed like some of these others. She loved Cape Breton. She tried hard to engage with people. As a person with a writing career, you root for her to succeed. But she still can't escape the fact that wherever she looks, she is applying a certain gaze.

There is a branch of philosophy called hermeneutics, and broadly speaking, it is the study of interpretation. It is the creation of understanding through the process of interpretation, or making sense of something.

We do not really look at anything in this world with innocent eyes. Everything we see is processed through a knowledge centre of information that we already have so that we can make sense of what we encounter, and it only makes sense to you, the person, via everything you already know. We can learn new things, we are always learning new things, but we are also always taking in information to be mostly understood within the limited parameters of the body of knowledge we already possess, that of the self.

You could not even go to Mars and be the first person on Mars without an idea of what it's going to be like when you get there because we all have information in our head about Mars even though no one has ever set foot on it. I hear it's red!

What I mean to say is, I think that Edna Staebler came and saw something she loved, and wrote as she saw fit. She wrote as she understood how to write about what she was seeing. She had knowledge of things like poor people, fishing villages, rural places, from everything that she had gathered in her life, and when she arrived in a village she had never been to before, she processed that information accordingly.

I think in some ways, she wrote the only book she could write. After all, what would she have encountered beforehand that was from the perspective of anyone there? Not much, maybe *Each Man's Son* by Hugh MacLennan.[35]

A cultural revival was going to happen that would produce writers I will talk about later, but at this point, it was still nascent. So, what else was Staebler going to write? She wrote what she knew.

Staebler's book made me think of working-class characters in Dickens because they often spoke in full phonetic accents, and because they were sympathetic characters, and because if you were a Canadian writer born in the early twentieth century like Staebler was, then I think that's what you have read. I do not think the decision to write phonetic speech for the working class or the poor comes out of nowhere; it is something you have seen before and learned that this is the way to do it.

George Orwell wrote an essay on how Dickens handled the working class in his books. They were similar writers in a sense. And he notes that even though Dickens has great admiration for the working class in his fiction writing, where he was a champion of the poor and oppressed, he nevertheless gives himself away in his memoirs. He was famous for having to work in a factory as a child when his father was in debtors' prison, and privately he wrote how much this hurt him. But what hurt the most was being as low as the other boys, and what gave him hope was being separated from them when the men would call him "the young gentleman."[36]

And so says Orwell, however much Dickens may admire the working classes, he does not wish to resemble them. And there it is—as much as you might admire, enjoy the company of, feel at home with the working class, these writers don't want to be them. Could never be them. The authenticity on the page is the author's alone.

If you gave someone from Neil's Harbour a chance to write a book about Staebler's three weeks visit to their village, would they write everything they say to sound different than what you sound like? Probably not. Would they introduce their village to the reader as "a desolate dump?" Doubtful. But they were also busy working, while she was there for three weeks of summer holiday, which is still the case in Cape Breton and everywhere in the rural Maritimes, places that burst with visitors all summer who muse at the lifestyle while everyone else is working, and often, specifically working for them.

And yet—on whose shelf is this fifty-year-old book still standing? I would say most of the book collections of the casual readers of Upper Canada (or wherever) have long dusted this one off the shelves. But I got it from a friend who had it in her bookstore in Cape Breton. Where people often pick up used copies with interest. And I do guarantee that people in Neil's Harbour have this book. They, most of all. Because we all want to be represented.

If you don't have people's authentic voice, then other people will come in to fill the gap. And if that is all you have to see yourself with, or if that is the majority of what you are going to get, then you will never feel fully realized and seen in the larger culture. You will always be a caricature of some kind passed through the lens of someone different, maybe someone who can't even help but feel better than you. And you know that is, consequently, how others will perceive you as well. When you look outside your small world, there will always be people looking back in at you. But to be beholden to what they think they see, or what they want to see, instead of being able to speak for yourself, is a terrible price just for having less.

// I said there was a cultural revival in the last part of the twentieth century in Cape Breton. There was a remarkable growth in regional consciousness. It is hard to give this a ground zero. It was the result of many factors and I do not think it was an uncommon thing for working-class places or any place at all in that time with the effects of modernization and globalization.

We had our coal strikes and labour leaders. We had television and radio and an influx of ideas and stories that showed what was possible. We had more students going to university than ever after the creation of the student loan program in the late 1960s. Government organizations were created with the arts in mind. We had sharp, homegrown satirical comedy that was wildly popular in the home circuit. The American counterculture came, both in the media and with a wave of actual draft dodgers. We had artists who moved in—ironically brought in by the popular imagination of Cape Breton as a place to escape modernity but oh well—people like Robert Frank, June Leaf, Philip Glass, Ken Nishi, Joan Jonas, Richard Serra, JoAnne Akalaitis. Music positively exploded onto the national stage. There was definitely something *happening* by the time I was born.

With that culture came writers. I want to take a few of them and talk about how they related to issues of class, speaking from my lifetime as an Islander. Alistair MacLeod, Rita Joe, Sheldon Currie, and Lynn Coady. Let's be clear though: this is only a selection. Cape Breton has always had writers and artists to tell their stories.

First of all, if I were to cast a net out over the country and ask what name comes to mind, it is hard to speak about Cape Breton literature without the mention of Alistair MacLeod. For some, he is synonymous with the island, though his subject matter is narrowly focused on one type of community. He wrote on a great deal of things—family, labour, culture, loss, love. When he wrote about characters who were hard rock miners, you knew it had something true behind it because he *was* a miner, before he was a professor.

Class was a concern of his from the very start. Take his short story "The Boat" from 1968. I had to read "The Boat" in high school.[37] It wasn't the Cape Breton that I knew, it was darker and emotionally colder and violent, but I knew the tourists who took pictures of people working, and I knew the terrible choice between staying or leaving for somewhere "better" only to break the heart of someone you love, or your own.

This was always going to be a concern of mine and everyone I knew. To stay or to leave. To leave, with opportunity and change but loss and grief, or to stay, to have home but be left behind and be poor and never knowing.

MacLeod's characters often deal with the dilemmas of class, and there are lines I never shook because they hit something so true to my community. True to that economic struggle, true to suffering the blows of capitalism that break apart your family or the things you know, because they are made irrelevant. But he was writing very specifically about the area of my community, so that makes sense. So, we will come back to him.

// In 1978 Rita Joe published her first collection of poems, including her most famous one, "I Lost My Talk."[38] This too is a school staple. She has the Order of Canada, and lines from this poem were included in the Truth and Reconciliation Commission's Report on Residential Schools in Canada:

I lost my talk
The talk you took away.
When I was a little girl
At Shubenacadie school.[39]

"I was only a housewife with a dream to bring laughter to the sad eyes of my people"—that is how Joe described herself.[40] But she was much more than that.

A few years ago I did a creative writing workshop with some high schoolers from Eskasoni—a reserve town where Joe lived many years of her life. Teenagers are terrifyingly silent in a group setting where you are trying to get them to share creative chatter, so there wasn't a lot forthcoming. However, after it was over, two friends from a group of three girls I had noticed came over to me and informed me that their other friend was ready to see me now. She was waiting outside, nervous but willing to recite a poem she wrote. And what did I think? she asked. I thought it was great. I thought it took great courage to did what she just did. And of course, Rita Joe came to mind, and of course, she said, she was one of her heroes.

It is maybe just a little easier to be courageous when one of the most famous poets was from your town. It tells you that your voice matters too. When I think of that girl, I hope she is still using that powerful voice, and I'm glad I got to hear it.

But more to the point, I hope that if she wants to be heard, there is a way for that to happen. That the barriers that normally exist for an author who is Indigenous and from a statistically impoverished community—two things that are related—are considered and mitigated by an industry that doesn't seem to see class. We celebrate Rita Joe, as we should, but do we make way for others like her?

In 1979 Sheldon Currie publishes *The Glace Bay Miners' Museum*.[41] This is only a few years after Staebler's *Cape Breton Harbour*, and when the characters speak, it is sometimes with a phonetic spelling of their accent. To highlight the fact that this is Glace Bay. There is a world of difference, though.

Currie is judicious with his use of the device. It does not show up on every page, and where it does, a local Cape Bretoner could hear that distinct Glace Bay sound. In other words, it makes sense. It contextualizes or territorializes. Looking at it I think, "I know what this is." It almost feels more *for* me, a local reader, than it does for an outside one. He didn't need to do it and other novels set in Glace Bay don't do it and get along fine. You'll never find Alistair MacLeod's characters talking in an accent, you'll hardly find them talking in contractions. (I'm joking.) Authors can have different styles of writing. But the fact is that the difference is clear. It wasn't the writing of accents I had a problem with, it was the *gaze*. Currie writes with a real authority, and it shows.

The Glace Bay Miners' Museum is funny and it is horrifying. It was written about a decade after the real Glace Bay Miners Museum opened to the public. Currie has a lot to say about the reality of mining vs. what the public can handle, can tolerate—will tolerate. The actual Miners Museum will take you into a mine, and it will give you a story that you can take. It is a family outing. It was created in celebration for Expo 67.

But the museum that Margaret MacNeil sets up in the story is different. MacNeil, and Currie, want visitors to look at the unbearable reality of the work. Her museum is grotesque and the events of her life are violent and tragic.

There will be other stories about the tragic side of life in a coal town after *The Glace Bay Miners' Museum*. It seems that this is what the culture has an appetite for, both within ourselves and without. It certainly seems that to be prestige, on the literary scene, you must open a wound. If you are poor, then you are miserable. But the culmination of these stories obscure the fact that places like Glace Bay, Sydney, or New Waterford were also functioning communities where many people had happy lives. Where they lived with great familiarity and camaraderie, played sports together, made music together, supported one another, laughed a lot, and missed it when it was gone.

As my uncle from Glace Bay would tell it to me, "You have to understand," he says, "these were men from different backgrounds, different religions, who would go down in a cart forty minutes into the darkest earth under the ocean to work together and be as brothers." The complex card game Tarabish, invented by Lebanese workers, is a symbol of Cape Breton identity, popularized in no small part by needing something to do in the cart that took workers underground from the surface and back, hours and hours a week. The miners had their own hockey league, it was called—what else—the Colliery hockey league. They would have to shower after every shift to get the coal dust off, and they would wash each other's backs. It is an intimate image. My father would tell me of the days when his cousins would visit from Glace Bay to where his own family lived in the countryside. His Aunt Veronica never showed up with only her own kids; the car would be full of the neighbours' kids as well, because it was a treat to get out to the country, and because that was the way in Glace Bay. Everyone belonged to everyone, and everyone was welcome.

I wish we had an appetite for all this as well, in stories.

I'm taking a detour now from literature, for a moment. Starting in the late 1980s/early 1990s, there was a rising interest in Cape Breton music on the national stage. It was music that was capturing people's attention to the area. My village was the home of the Rankin Family, and you'd often see them on TV in the '90s. Or John Allan Cameron, whose career started earlier. It is much easier to imagine yourself as a success when you turn on the TV and someone from your hometown is on it. Rita MacNeil from Big Pond had a show as well, and Rita was just an absolute icon of the island. What's more, you'd often see her with the Men of the Deeps, a choral group of coal miners who sang with their pit hats on. The full regalia of their class. And they sang about coal mining, on national television.

Though it must be said—do you think, for instance, a Black working-class choir or song group would be afforded the same television coverage at that time? I don't. We were lucky to have that representation as much as we were part of a system that provided it.

But at the time, I thought everyone in Canada watched regional shows that were specific to them. When I asked my husband, an Albertan, what he had to watch as a kid, I was expecting some kind of analogue of what we had, but no, he had to watch *Rita and Friends* just like we did. No *Ian Tyson and the Sour Gas Plant Choir*, I guess. So, it is funny that for a brief moment, during the worst time economically, and most devastating time for communities in decades, Cape Breton culture was being broadcast the way it was. I don't have an answer for it, but I am sure I benefitted from it.

Now back to books.

In 1998 Lynn Coady's career takes off with the novel *Strange Heaven*.[42] Coady was a new kind of writer coming out of Atlantic Canada. She was funny and angry and young and a woman, and in various works she is interrogating what she thinks and what you think about Cape Breton. Both Cape Breton as a living region and as an idea in people's minds.

Coady grew up in Port Hawkesbury in the 1980s, which was, as she puts it, "a shit time" to grow up in Port Hawkesbury. This was a paper mill town that had seen better days. I also know Port Hawkesbury well. It was bigger than the little villages, but it was only an hour down the road, and the paper mill had the best jobs. You were doing good if you got on there.

So, when Coady started writing stories set at home, it was exciting and it was present. The word "gritty" gets used a lot. "It was gritty." But I think it's more that she just didn't hold back. She portrayed people in a way that she knew, and if you lived there, you knew people like that too.

There is nothing surprising here in the people we meet, only recognition. Poor people from the working class. They get to be no more or less complicated or disappointing than anyone anywhere else. If your mental image of the Maritimes was one of stereotyped pleasantness, then yes, I suppose you would find it gritty, but I think that reaction is telling. It is unsettling to have an image overturned.

In her 2000 short story "A Great Man's Passing," I see some of the class issues that I've mulled on in life cracked open and examined.[43] A grandfather has died, the titular "Man." The narrator lives at home with the rest of the poor side of the family. Wealthier, culturally distant cousins travel in for the funeral from Ontario and Boston.

A rich American employs the narrator, he loves it in Cape Breton, he came to retire there and he is oblivious to the hardship around him. On TV, men grovel for work with humiliating familiarity. The house that opens the story is falling apart but lots of people live in it. There is impotent anger and guilt in the air because things just aren't better than they are.

Yet you can't help but laugh when someone at the bar the narrator works at yells "foit!"—F-O-I-T—(again I love the perfectly deployed accents) and the horrified American looks on while two locals kick each other in the head outside to a delighted crowd.

Perhaps the worst commentary is saved for the characters who are almost Cape Bretoners themselves. The better-off cousins from away, who only come to visit once a year or every few years, but when they do come, they come with their romantic notions of what Cape Breton is.

They playact, they put on accents they don't have, they laugh loud, drink local beer, listen to fiddly folk music, go to square dances, and pretend they are from a place they were never from. They believe the grandfather was "a great man" when he was an ordinary decrepit old man if anything, and they put the Folk gaze on everything around them, because that is what they want this place to be, not what it is. And this is family.

One of Coady's strengths is disassembling what anyone thinks the family ought to look like and behave. This is particularly savage, in my opinion, because we all have those cousins from away who are more "Cape Breton" than even we were. We have all encountered people who come back and do this. And as I said, when you are always faced with that choice of staying or leaving and what it will mean for your life, or your children's lives, here is this powerful spectre in this story that I think no one is unaware of but no one explicitly talks about. That you or yours will become one of these distant, grasping, unmoored relatives in the story, that you know she pulled from life. With all your money, and not a clue.

In 1999 Alistair MacLeod—he's back!—publishes his one novel, *No Great Mischief*.[44] It was a very big deal at the time. The master's masterwork. International acclaim. Class struggle was at its heart.

But I learned a lesson very early on from this book about how people read. That once a book is out of your hands, it's gone, and it becomes whatever other people say it is. And if we are talking in terms of class, you could write the very soul of your experience on a page and someone could read it and still see something completely different because that was never their life.

You can't control what people read even when the words are on the page in front of them.

I was still in high school when *No Great Mischief* came out. I remember my mother reading it, and that she could not put it down. "It's just like my own relatives," she said. She was seeing herself in this book in a real way, in a rare way to her. I know one thing that stood out to her was the way that the older brothers of the protagonist in the book lived.

They're poor, they live alone, they're rural, they play the card game Auction, they live very rough. They sleep in their clothes and use overcoats for makeshift extra blankets. A horse pulls someone's rotten tooth out that was tied to a string. It was so cold in their house that they would wake up to frost on the inside of the walls. They never had cups where the handles weren't broken, or they drank their tea from jam jars. And they were alcoholics.

My mother saw pieces of her uncles here, or people she knew, and the frost-covered nails in the farmhouse of her own life. As I grew older myself, there were some people in my own life who seemed to walk out of this book, but of course it was only because MacLeod had tapped into something like a pure vein of experiences common enough among people like me. In my own uncle's Ontario apartment only months ago at the time of writing this, I remembered *No Great Mischief*.

Yet I remember another thing that happened that summer in high school when the book came out. I walked up to a tourist who was looking for directions. She had rolled down her car window. This was the year 2000, before GPS.

"And do you speak Gaelic?" she asked me.

"A little," I said.

"Oh my god," I recall her saying almost to herself, pulling her head back in the car. "I just got here and I already met one of them."

With that, she drove off. I stood there stunned for a moment. But I knew one thing for sure, she had read *No Great Mischief*. I knew this because I worked at the museum in the village and I knew who came that summer because of that book. It had brought in tourists. And for her, and some others, it was like we had read two different books.

What was so real, and raw, to my mother, was romantic and selective to a different audience. The painfully sharp, specific working-class portrait carved by MacLeod for my mom was a soft thing seen from a distance for these others, and standing there I felt like something to be seen on a human safari. She didn't read that book and remember the cold in the morning where you could see your breath in the house. She never felt that cold, it was a fantasy. Now I don't know that woman. Maybe she comes from a family of hard-rock miners who know the violence of that job and social forces that put you there when other people would never do that work. But it did not feel like it.

You don't have to be from the same class to understand a book. We ought to read books from people of all different backgrounds than ourselves; it will make us a better society. But that was where I learned that you can't help what people see because we all read books in our own way, and we all make sense of what we take in based on who we are already.

You have to try, though. And maybe what I'm really talking about is just another way of saying that we need is more art from working-class artists so that things stop feeling like a fantasy, and are realities that we accept instead.

// Now I would like to, in this last part, talk about my own experience directly.

My 2022 graphic novel *Ducks* was a memoir that dealt with many realities of the working class through the eyes of my twenty-one-year-old self, working in the oil sands of Alberta.[45]

It is over four hundred pages of comics that comment on a number of things. Class among them. Also gender, corporate and government power, labour, money, how we treat each other in isolation, mental health, drug abuse, sexual violence, Indigenous health, environmental concerns— there were many things that I tried to address but every- thing had to be true to the experience and viewpoint of my younger, inexperienced self.

Even though I try to present an even picture with co-workers who joke around and moments of levity, the book is often heavy. There is sexual assault, there are moments of despair. There is addiction and racism and indifference. There is a hard look at an industry and a life that a lot of people have never had to think about.

And in *Ducks*, I have portrayed an industry that has touched the lives of so many people from my home. The oil sands took people away, made empty desks in the schools, familiar faces disappeared from the streets, lifted fathers from their families, it was such a common story—all in the name of getting ahead. It seemed like the only option in a place where there was nothing. And if you knew Cape Breton at the time, then you know what I am talking about.

I don't know how it was for other age groups, but for mine, for my coming of age in Cape Breton, identity felt something of a Janus face, depending on who was assessing you.

Whatever the truth of it, newspaper and television reports often showed what looked like an industrial waste-land. The tar ponds in Sydney became famous for being the largest toxic waste site in North America. People were getting sick. Unemployment was rife. Buildings were boarded up, smoke choked the air, dirty-faced men in hard hats went into dirty-looking jobs that they said they were desperate to keep. People were often angry on TV, and interviews with them highlighted their regional accents that the rest of the country found funny, a joke. After all, as sad as it was, everyone else wanted these industries shut down. They were too expensive to subsi-dize and limp along with taxpayer money, they were outdated, they should have been gone years ago.

On the flip side, you have just as strong of an image in the tourist industry that promoted Cape Breton as a bucolic musical paradise. Around every corner, a vista of green and blue, a fiddler, a fishing boat, a dream. Here the accents delight, and the island beguiles and enchants. In this one, you (the Islander) are the Folk of Ian McKay, and there are no smokestacks, and the tour-ists are told not to go to Sydney.

I am not from Industrial Cape Breton, the coal mines and Sydney Steel and the tar ponds. I am from the rural side being sold to tourists. But everyone in my family and my community and the rural areas has worked in or has family connections to mining, to factory work, to industry, whether that was in Industrial Cape Breton, in Windsor, Sudbury, Elliot Lake, Detroit, Fort McMurray, or wherever you had to go, because the face of rural life is only a face. The reality is more complex.

There was a documentary in the 1970s called the *Vanishing Cape Breton Fiddler* that made the case that all the fiddlers had disappeared from the island, but they hadn't really. The best ones were just all working at Chrysler's car plant in Windsor, Ontario.[46]

How bizarre to have these two images competing for the mask you wear in public, depending which one people see when you tell them you are from Cape Breton. I have had people light up, charmed, and I have had people immediately look down on me, and, of course, I have had many people not know where in the hell that is at all.

Ducks begins in 2005, when I graduated university. But I graduated high school in 2001, and this was a particularly rough time in Cape Breton history. They were shutting every industry down, and the communities suffered. Everything was going—the pulp mill in Port Hawkesbury, Sydney Steel, the last coal mines on the island; my school was razed to the ground, even the post offices were closing. The grocery store that employed my father had changed hands about three times in the past few years, and it was the only store left in town. Everything felt untenable.

When I was in grade eleven, the last year before they closed the school, there were twenty-three kids in my grade, and there were seven children in grade primary. It was like the population was just going off a cliff in a matter of years. We were told to leave, just leave, there is nothing for you here. There was a sense that other young people were living out a life of options and you were eking out the sputtering death of a statistic in what happens in "these places."

So, I left.

And so, you would be forgiven for thinking that my story is one of net cultural loss, if you read *Ducks* and felt a hole somewhere inside, I can't blame you for that; it is a difficult read.

It is a disservice to my community to let you think that way, though. So, I want to close this talk with my beautiful truth. That truth being that I am here today with a career as an artist, as a cartoonist, a writer, the whole nine yards, because I am the beneficiary of a long history of a community that values art. And that is a working-class legacy also. Art for no money, art for each other, art for shared history, for storytelling, for pleasure, art through hard times, art because it has value. In the working class, your body of labour is what it is: If there are not many options, then the job that is available is good and you have to take it. Your body has to take it. But your mind is a different story.

In my life, I may have lacked confidence as anyone might, and I might have worried that I was not as good as other people, or that I would pale compared to those with more resources. But I never once questioned the value of my mind, and that is the gift of my community. Even as I shipped my body out for unforgiving labour, I never felt like my voice wasn't worth something.

Story is what we are all about, isn't it. I have been telling you a story about Cape Breton for a while now. So, let me tell you a different one.

First of all, I should mention something about my culture, in my small part of the province. The past couple of decades have seen newcomers bring a greater wealth of cultural diversity to the area, but in my childhood, it was predominantly the culture of the settler Gael. There is still a strong presence of that culture now. People of Scottish descent, but not Scottish. Of course, they were not the only ones. There has been a sizeable Dutch population since the Second World War, there are names of Loyalist origin, to the north and south you will find Acadian communities, and to the east, Mi'kmaq communities. But in the enclave of communities from which I hail, there is a strong Gaelic presence, and that is the culture I claim. So, I speak for myself.

That tourism industry we have talked about so much built heavily on the romanticized version of these people. The tartans, the bagpipes, the mysticism, and the dominance of this image at the expense of, and purposeful erasure of, other cultures, especially if they were not white. And it worked. Tartanism is hard to shake.

But it was a package created for the consumption of the white middle class and foreign visitors who wanted to see kilts and had a mania for Bonnie Prince Charlie and Robbie Burns. It made caricatures of the actual people, who never heard of Robbie Burns Day and never owned a kilt. Their language, Gaelic, was not a sellable commodity the way the image of a bagpiper was, so it was left to die on the vine.

Anything that could not go on the shortbread cookie tin—a commodified, tourist shop version of culture—was not important, and anything that could be serviceable to that cookie-tin vision of a sellable image was amplified, sometimes invented, and slapped on. And it is still hard for people to separate the cartoon tartanism version of Gaelic Nova Scotia with its commercial interests and its racial discomfort and its cringe and its ubiquity, and the living people, who have a culture and a history and are not a fabrication of a corporate or conservative interest.

When I speak of my culture, I know I am contending with this image. So, I thought I would state that outright because we have been talking so much about all this.

And I am contending with Ian McKay. McKay was so focused on taking down "the Folk" and his book was so popular that I think he helped create an atmosphere where depictions of rural settler cultures that aren't explicitly doing their bit to sufficiently upend the Folk narrative are received with suspicion.

"There never were any Folk," says McKay. "There were only the categories and vigorously redescribed if not invented traditions that enabled us to think there were."[47]

People in *Quest of the Folk* are never not under the gaze of commodification of some kind. They never exist for themselves. If it looks quaint to the outsider, flag it, put it in the Cultural Construction bin.

But there were real people and real cultures here long before the folklorists and tourist industry. More came after. Nova Scotia is diverse and full of as much cultural truth for itself alone as it has been subject to, or even participated in, cultural construction for others.

Do you remember the poet Aonghas from earlier, my great, great, great-grandfather? The one who wrote the poem about the crop failure in the mid 1800s. He was not the only poet around then.

I mentioned his mentor, the locally famous Allan "the Ridge" MacDonald. MacDonald wrote a poem one time, he spent the night at his neighbour's house. When he woke in the morning it was to the sound of a woman named Catherine singing to a baby in another room. Her grandchild. Lying there, listening, he would write a poem in her praise. In the poem, he writes that he awoke to the steady, tranquil sound of her voice, which enthralled his mind and gladdened his heart. How true a friend she was, cheerful, singing to the child, a more beautiful sound than the birds on tips of branches or of any stringed instrument. He praises her manner, her dignity, her husband and family, and in the end, he says, "I am well able to relate this, they were my good friends." It's beautiful.[48]

Catherine, I have her name these generations later. She is my great, great, great, great-grandmother. She should be lost to time for all that her station in life was. She could not read or write, she was a small woman, she had not a word of English. But she comes alive because the poetry of her people was a poetry of community. And aren't I fortunate for that? That is a treasure, for me, to know the ways beauty, love, and connection have always been a part of life. People really like to punt around their opinions on Gaelic, but it is for me to decide how much this means to me, this is mine, and it means a lot.

Here's another story.

I was always jealous of the musicians because musical talent was such a prize. There were famous fiddle players and the like. You might know some famous names yourself, but it's only recently that music became a career anyone could do. Until twenty years ago, even the most genius of musicians either worked at something else or lived in poverty if they were driven to do nothing but make music. But they were revered as legends. They *were* legends. They knew more about music than you could imagine. Not just how to play it, but how to make it, the lore around it, they could tell the style from one village to another where you only heard the same sound.

They would say that music was "in you," that it followed a lineage, that it was in your family, that it was natural.

It didn't *have* to be, but it was often found in families—
a particular talent. Fiddlers, piano players, singers, and
dancers cropping up like carrots in a patch. We are not
the only Beatons around, there are plenty of Beatons,
and some of them are, famously, musical Beatons. Alas,
not mine.

It was still something special for music and dance to
be so treasured, even if I had two left feet and fiddles
and pianos turned to dust in my hands. I brought my
future husband to his first square dance at one point
when he was visiting me years ago. Rite of passage, you
might say. The crowd was chatting and the news was
that Joe Rankin was back home, and there was antic-
ipation that he was going to dance. You see, there is
one point in the square dance where the floor clears
completely and the best of the dancers step in one by
one to do some steps. It's like a showcase, and everyone
else is jammed along the walls watching the massive
empty floor with a lone dancer.

At last, that part of the night came up and Joe Rankin
stepped up to dance. People are pumped. My husband
turned to me and said, "Is that him?" and I said yes.
The man everyone had been waiting for was a man in
his fifties, who looked like he worked in construction.
Because he does work in construction. He was wearing
white pants, like you do when people are going to look at
your legs. And if my husband was a little confused, the
people around us breathed, "God, he was always such a
good dancer, like his mother, ach, it was in his people."

I like that story because Rankin works in construction
in Alberta. His body reflects his years of labour, that is
his life. But at home, his value, his history, is the music in
him, so much that they clear the floor for him. Again, it's
beautiful. I love it. I don't even think I would have noticed

there was anything special about it if my husband wasn't there to point it out, why this unconventional man should be a star that night. But he was.

We had so much art around us, in different forms. Wit and humour were prized. When I was interviewed about making humour comics, people often asked, "Where did the humour come from?" and I always said, "home," though it was hard to get into it. How do you explain humour? All you knew at a young age was that you wanted to be as funny as the people around you. You wanted them to notice you.

Linden MacIntyre put it this way: "Every kid grows up wanting the favourable attention of an adult, and the best way to get that is to play the fiddle. If you can't play the fiddle, you have to tell a story. So there's an oral tradition, passed between generations, embedded in stories from simple, ordinary lives. Turning that into something that holds attention puts a high premium on clever speech and humour. You learn to embellish anecdotes from daily living and make them entertaining enough that people remember you."[49] MacIntyre knows what he is talking about. I was making a career in comics already by the time his second novel, *The Bishop's Man*, won the Giller Prize.[50] I do not think it was a surprise to anyone, but there was pride. We had all watched him host an acclaimed national investigative news program, *The Fifth Estate*, for as long as I could remember, and never lose his accent. When his writing career took off to similar acclaim, a national award felt like giving the king his flowers. But I like this quote about where storytelling comes from, culturally. I recognize it. He's only from down the road.

If you were good with humour, you could be almost immortal. Believe me when I say that people stop me—even only days ago someone did in the grocery store—to tell me something funny my grandparent said one time, people who died in 1994 or 1986. They do it just because they remember and thought I'd like to know, and I do, I do want to know. Maybe we didn't get the music in my family, but we had the stories and the humour and everyone knew it, and that made me feel like I had it and I could do it. And so, I did. Confidence in numbers, through time. Affirmation. It was a way of being seen.

When I was a teenager working in that museum in my village, we were visited all the time by people looking for their ancestors. A name, a story, a location. But they were sometimes searching for something more than that. They were searching for something inside of themselves that they felt was lost to time and distance. Connection. Identity. Everything we took for granted because you can't throw a stone without hitting a fiddler and you can't tell a story without including six people known by a nickname and a patronym three names long that everyone completely understands. I have a family of cousins where some go by the patronym and some by the nickname. Donald Angus A., Joey Angus A., Dougal Angus A., and Jack Stretch. Confusing? Not at all. Jack is tall and slim. It makes perfect sense.

Stories, music, poetry, dance, humour, all these things kept a tiny corner of the world connected through generations. I am informed and enriched by it. It is about finding value in each other and so in yourself. It gives you strength. Or, to borrow from my musical kin, it is mellifluous. It is to be in tune with something. I liked living in the big cities of the world, I enjoyed it very much. But I moved home eventually because I know myself here. I feel like a version of myself that I like the most. Other people also know me, and they may know generations before me also. And when I tell a story, I am pulling from the strength of something deep inside. Of a woman who can't read or write, singing to her grandbaby in the early morning with clear and beautiful voice. A man who is poor and keeps a sense of humour about it in poetry and song. A revered dancer with a body of a construction worker. A fiddler who is a composer and a genius, pulled from the middle of making the hay to play at a wedding. A cartoonist who wants to be as funny as the people around her, and tells stories because who I am is who we are. I write, I make art, I know who I am, and I am grateful for the story within my community that taught me that I had a voice that mattered. That culture belonged to me, with power and authenticity, as it should to us all.

Thank you.

Notes

1. E.P. Thompson, *The Making of the English Working Class* (Penguin Books, 2013), 12.

2. Canada Council for the Arts, Department of Canadian Heritage, and Ontario Arts Council, *A Statistical Profile of Artists in Canada in 2016* (Canada Council for the Arts, November 27, 2019), https://canadacouncil.ca/research/ research-library/2019/03/a-statistical-profile-of-artists- in-canada-in-2016.

3. Karina Palmitesta, *Results of the 2022 Canadian Book Publishing Diversity Baseline Survey* (Association of Canadian Publishers, 2023), https://publishers.ca/ wp-content/uploads/2023/02/230123-Diversity- Baseline-Survey-Report-FINAL.pdf.

4. See Sean Speer, Sosina Bezu, and Renze Nauta, *Canada's New Working Class* (Cardus, September 29, 2022), https://www.cardus.ca/research/work-economics/ reports/canadas-new-working-class/.

5. Shannon Proudfoot, "What Does It Mean to Be Working Class in Canada?" *Maclean's*, July 16, 2019, https://www. macleans.ca/society/ what-does-it-mean-to-be-working-class-in-canada/.

6. Angus Reid Institute, *Canadians & Class: Strong Belief in Canada as a Meritocracy, But Plurality Identify as the Same Social Class as Their Parents,* September 21, 2023, https://angusreid.org/great-canadian-class-study/.

7. Karol Jan Borowiecki, "The Origins of Creativity: The Case of the Arts in the United States since 1850," *Trinity Economics Papers* (February 2019), https://ideas.repec. org/p/tcd/tcduee/tep0219.html.

8. Quoctrung Bui, "A Secret of Many Urban 20-Somethings: Their Parents Help with the Rent," *New York Times*, February 9, 2017, https://www.nytimes.com/2017/02/09/ upshot/a-secret-of-many-urban-20-somethings-their- parents-help-with-the-rent.html.

9.   You can read some of my archived comics at http://www.
     harkavagrant.com/.

10. Charles Haight Farnham, "Cape Breton Folk," *Harper's New
     Monthly Magazine*, March 1886, repr. in Stephen F.
     Spencer, "Cape Breton Folk," *Acadiensis* 8, no. 2 (1979):
     90–106, https://www.jstor.org/stable/30302653.

11. Farnham, "Cape Breton Folk," 102.

12. Petition from the Mi'kmaq at Whycocomagh regarding
     white men taking over their lands, 1855, Nova Scotia
     House of Assembly—Assembly petitions series, Nova
     Scotia Archives, RG 5, series P, vol. 15, no. 9, Halifax,
     https://archives.novascotia.ca/mikmaq/archives/?ID=526.

13. Petition of several inhabitants of Whycocomagh regarding
     lands granted to Mi'kmaq, 1857, Nova Scotia House of
     Assembly—Assembly petitions series, Nova Scotia
     Archives, RG 5, series P, vol. 16, no. 47, Halifax, https://
     archives.novascotia.ca/mikmaq/archives/?ID=527.

14. Canada Council, *A Statistical Profile*.

15. Palmitesta, *Results*, 12.

16. Statistics Canada, "The Canadian Census: A Rich Portrait
     of the Country's Religious and Ethnocultural Diversity,"
     The Daily, October 26, 2022, https://www150.statcan.
     gc.ca/n1/daily-quotidien/221026/dq221026b-eng.htm.

17. Statistics Canada, "Canadian Census."

18. Palmitesta, *Results*, 12.

19. Palmitesta, *Results*, 25.

20. Òrain Aonghais 'ic Alasdair, *The Songs of Angus
     MacDonald*, collected and translated by Effie Rankin (pub.
     by author, 2021), 8–10. Used with permission.

21. Ian McKay, *The Quest of the Folk: Antimodernism and
     Cultural Selection in Twentieth-Century Nova Scotia*
     (McGill-Queen's University Press, 1994).

22. For Creighton's publication history, see "Books by Helen,"
     at https://www.helencreighton.org/books-by-helen-
     creighton/.

23. McKay, *Quest*, 26.

24. For some of Asch's work, see Douglas Harper, *Cape Breton 1952: The Photographic Vision of Timothy Asch* (International Visual Sociology Association, 1994), 12.

25. Edna Staebler, *Cape Breton Harbour* (McClelland & Stewart, 1972).

26. Edna Staebler, *Food That Really Schmecks* (McGraw-Hill Ryerson, 1968).

27. Edna Staebler, "Duellists of the Deep," *Maclean's*, July 15, 1948, 18, 46–47.

28. Staebler, *Cape Breton Harbour*, 13.

29. Staebler, *Cape Breton Harbour*, 17.

30. Pierre Berton quoted in "Edna Staebler—A Writer's Life Rooted in Community," The Working Centre, accessed September 6, 2024, https://www.theworkingcentre.org/past-mayors-dinner-guests-honour/7090-edna-staebler-writer%E2%80%99s-life-rooted-community.

31. Veronica Ross, *To Experience Wonder: Edna Staebler: A Life* (Dundurn Press, 2003), 106.

32. Margaret Warner Morley, *Down North and Up Along* (Dodd, Mead & Co., 1900).

33. Arthur Walworth, *Cape Breton, Isle of Romance* (Longmans, Green & Co., 1948).

34. Paul J.C. Friedlander, "Pointers for a Holiday, in Town and Country," *New York Times*, August 1, 1948, https://timesmachine.nytimes.com/timesmachine/1948/08/01/86751366.html.

35. Hugh MacLennan, *Each Man's Son* (Macmillan, 1951).

36. George Orwell, "Charles Dickens," in *Inside the Whale and Other Essays* (Victor Gollancz, 1940), 45.

37. Alistair MacLeod, *Island: The Collected Short Stories of Alistair MacLeod* (McClelland & Stewart, 2000).

38. Rita Joe, *Poems of Rita Joe* (Abanaki Press, 1978).

39. Rita Joe, "I Lost My Talk," in Truth and Reconciliation Commission of Canada, *Canada's Residential Schools: The Legacy*, vol. 5 of *The Final Report of the Truth and Reconciliation Commission of Canada* (McGill-Queen's University Press, 2015), 106, https://ehprnh2mwo3.

exactdn.com/wp-content/uploads/2021/01/Volume_5_
Legacy_English_Web.pdf.

40. From the book jacket for Rita Joe, *We Are the Dreamers:
    Recent and Early Poetry* (Breton Books, 1999), quoted at
    https://mikmawarchives.ca/documents/
    we-are-the-dreamers-recent-and-early-poetry.

41. Sheldon Currie, *The Glace Bay Miners' Museum* (Deluge
    Press, 1979).

42. Lynn Coady, *Strange Heaven* (Anchor Canada, 1998).

43. Lynn Coady, *Play the Monster Blind* (Vintage Canada,
    2001).

44. Alistair MacLeod, *No Great Mischief*, new ed. (Vintage,
    2001).

45. Kate Beaton, *Ducks: Two Years in the Oil Sands* (Drawn &
    Quarterly, 2022).

46. Charles Reynolds, dir., *Vanishing Cape Breton Fiddler*,
    aired on CJCB–Channel 4, the CBC affiliate in Sydney, on
    January 6, 1972. See Marie Thompson, "The Myth of the
    Vanishing Cape Breton Fiddler: The Role of a CBC Film in
    the Cape Breton Fiddle Revival," *Acadiensis* 35, no. 2
    (2006), https://journals.lib.unb.ca/index.php/Acadiensis/
    article/view/10596.

47. McKay, *Quest*, 302.

48. Effie Rankin, *As a' Braighe / Beyond the Braes: The Gaelic
    Songs of Allan the Ridge MacDonald* (Cape Breton
    University Press, 2005), 85.

49. Karalee Clerk, "If You Can't Play the Fiddle, You Have to Tell
    a Story," *Atlantic Books*, no. 90 (2019), https://
    atlanticbooks.ca/stories/if-you-cant-play-the-fiddle-you-
    have-to-tell-a-story/.

50. Linden MacIntyre, *The Bishop's Man* (Random House
    Canada, 2009).

CLC Kreisel Lecture Series

Published by University of Alberta Press and the
Centre for Literatures in Canada / Centre de littératures au Canada